What Others Are Saying . . .

"I am so grateful for your disposition to help during the hardest times. Thanks to the support of the ROW Foundation we were able to provide care and antiepileptic drugs to many patients in PUERTO RICO following the devastation caused by Hurricane Maria."

Ignacio Pita, MD, FAES
Director, Puerto Rico Comprehensive Epilepsy Program

....

"ROW helped us bring EEG equipment to a rural hospital in Kenya. It also provides an ongoing supply of Roweepra for our work in HAITI in places where antiepileptic drugs aren't available. I'm encouraged by the spirit and action of ROW and look forward to partnering with them in the future."

Peter London, MD
Founder & Director, International Neurology Services

....

"The contribution ROW is making to the people of SIERRA LEONE is substantial. By offering medications consistently without interruption, it significantly benefits those with epilepsy and helps strengthen the country's health system. We appreciate ROW's service and look forward to an ongoing partnership."

Benjamin Parra
Executive Director, Healey International Relief Foundation

....

"We've benefitted from ROW through a grant of EEG equipment to the Armenia League Against Epilepsy and through ongoing medication grants to Arabkir Pediatric Hospital in Yerevan, ARMENIA. You have changed some lives and literally saved others. We are very thankful for the work of ROW around the world."

Biayna Sukhudyan, MD
Chief of Neurology, Arabkir Pediatric Hospital

What Others Are Saying . . .

"ROW provided funds for educational materials used in training EEG technicians in ETHIOPIA. We so appreciate ROW's focus, not only on serving people with epilepsy in under-resourced areas but in helping build capacity within those areas for more comprehensive, long-term solutions."

Teguo Djoyum Daniel, BS, CNIM, R.EEG.T
President, Global Organization of Health Education

....

"The needs of epilepsy patients in ZAMBIA are very great. Access to anti-seizure medication, particularly in rural areas, is often difficult and many health facilities experience erratic supply of essential antiepileptic drugs. I am pleased the ROW Foundation is working to address these needs around the world, and I look forward to the good that can be done here in Zambia."

Sr. Ornella Ciccone, MD
Consulting Neuropediatrician, Ndola, Zambia

....

"With a grant from the ROW Foundation, we were able to provide Puente de Solidaridad in BOLIVIA with anti-seizure medications for its epilepsy program in Cochabamba. We are thankful for that initial grant and for ROW's commitment to providing an ongoing, sustainable supply of medication.

Kurt Florian
Board of Directors, Solidarity Bridge

....

"The ROW Foundation's medication grant to our clinic in Jacmel is allowing us to better treat our patients with epilepsy. Their lives have been drastically improved. The folks at ROW are good to work with and we are grateful for their strategic partnership in the fight against epilepsy in HAITI.

Jared McCrory
Executive Director, Children's Hope

What Others Are Saying . . .

"ROW's strategy of leveraging business profits to provide care for the global poor in a category that would otherwise remain unaddressed—like those we work with in INDIA—is sheer brilliance."

Robb Hansen
Executive Director, Emmanuel Hospital Association, USA

. . . .

"Even in nations that enjoy the finest in medical care, under-resourced populations can and do exist. We appreciate the medication grants that ROW has made available that have allowed us to serve people who otherwise would have fallen through the cracks. Many thanks!"

Ben Slack
Executive Director, Epilepsy Foundation of North/Central Illinois

One World
One Standard

BY MIKE HAMEL

ALSO BY MIKE HAMEL

The Entrepreneur's Creed
Executive Influence
Giving Back
Stumbling Toward Heaven: My Cancer Journey
We Will Be Landing Shortly: Now What?

Matterhorn the Brave series:
The Sword and the Flute
Talis Hunters
Pyramid Scheme
Jewel Heist
Dragon's Tale
Rylan the Renegade
Tunguska Event
The Book of Stories
www.MatterhornTheBrave.com

TLC series:
UFO on the Rez
Bezer's Billions
The Long Walk Home
Zack's Cavern
The Green Bees
www.TLCstories.com

Lizzy the Leatherback
Queen Quillaabee

65,000,000

MORE THAN
65 MILLION PEOPLE
ARE LIVING WITH EPILEPSY WORLDWIDE

80%

Live in low and middle
income countries

75%

Do NOT receive
treatment

To the visionaries behind OWP and
ROW who are creating a brighter
future for millions of people.

———
and to
———

Bloncie
(2003 - 2018)
Port-au-Prince, Haiti
Determined, joyful, and friendly,
a sobering reminder that helping
others can never happen too soon.

Contents

The Vision

Big Pharma (the nickname for large pharmaceutical companies) is a trillion-dollar industry dominated by a handful of international corporations. They make obscene profits in the United States and a handful of other wealthy countries. According to a 2016 Gallup Poll, only the federal government is held in lower esteem by most Americans. "The pharmaceutical industry last year registered its worst showing in the 16 years that Gallup has been tracking how different sectors are perceived," reported Ed Silverman for STAT. "The pharmaceutical industry actually has a 'net positive' rating of negative 23."

It's surprising, then, that a new social enterprise model would arise from this milieu that could become a global game changer.

Scott Boyer spent three decades carving out a successful career in Big Pharma. He began right out of college with Abbott Laboratories, then moved onto Bristol-Myers Squibb. He wound up as a consultant with InVentiv Health. While doing research on the global sales of various products, Scott noticed a disturbing trend.

The more he investigated, the more troubled he became.

"One day I was analyzing market research data about a new drug," Scott recalls. "The wealthy and emerging markets were grouped together on the charts and graphs. Then there was this small, lonely bar on the far end of the chart titled 'ROW.' It stood for 'Rest Of World.'"

"The more I studied the data, the more I noticed the glaring discrepancy. Big Pharma focused almost exclusively on the wealthiest countries: the US, Japan, some EU nations and a few others. The other 175 or 180 countries got lumped together in ROW and largely ignored. There's not enough profit potential in these places."

Internalizing the data, Scott imagined how unfortunate it would be to be someone with a significant disease like epilepsy in a ROW country. Because of politics and economics, he would never have access to proper diagnosis and drugs. This insight, and the sense of injustice it stirred, led to the ROW Foundation.

The vision for ROW is simple: One World. One Standard. It's based on the premise that epilepsy patients in under-resourced areas should have the same opportunity for treatment as patients in the developed world. Instead, they go without the diagnostic tools, effective treatments, and basic medications we take for granted.

My heart breaks over all the potential that goes untapped because these people can't get the care needed to improve their lives, care that's readily available elsewhere.

"The social and economic impact on patients and their families is devastating," Scott continues. "My heart breaks over all the potential that goes untapped because these people can't get the care needed to improve their lives, care that's readily available elsewhere."

ROW is not a typical nonprofit. Scott and his partner, Bruce Duncan, created the foundation in 2014 in tandem with a start-up company, One World Pharmaceuticals. OWP is a for-profit company that makes effective and inexpensive epilepsy medications. Profits from the business underwrite the foundation.

Bruce and Scott met at church. They soon discovered they had a lot in common. At this stage in their careers, both men wanted to move from success to significance. Bruce, a CPA with a law degree from Case Western, had worked at the executive level in large corporations. As he listened to Scott's burden about ROW, he thought of a hybrid business model adopted by an organization with which he was familiar, Tyndale House Publishing.

Bruce shared the model with Scott, who loved the concept. "At its core, it's rather straightforward," Scott later wrote:

> A nonprofit (ROW) holds a significant shareholder stake in a for-profit business (OWP). When the for-profit makes money, it pays dividends to its shareholders and the nonprofit gets its share. Since the nonprofit is an invested strategic partner, it's difficult to

sell the for-profit without the nonprofit's approval. If the for-profit is sustainable and scalable, it will provide ongoing revenues for the nonprofit to carry out its humanitarian mission.

Funding for the nonprofit doesn't come in the form of charitable giving at the whim of the for-profit business. Rather, the for-profit business becomes the financial engine that drives the nonprofit. As the business thrives, so does the nonprofit.

OWP isn't research driven. It doesn't have the high cost of developing new drugs but specializes in branded generics. Its lean business structure is designed to provide steady and strong support for its philanthropic vision.

With the organizational pieces in place, Scott and Bruce set about finding the right person to head the ROW Foundation. This person would be on its board, with Scott as Chair, but they needed a point person who shared their passion. In early 2014, they approached Dr. Paul Regan with the opportunity.

Paul had thirty years of experience in nonprofits. After earning his EdD in nonprofit leadership from the University of Massachusetts at Lowell, he'd served as CEO, CFO, and COO of various philanthropic and international relief organizations.

"I had served with Bruce on a nonprofit board in the 1990s," Paul says. "When he and Scott outlined the model for OWP and ROW, I got very excited. The clarity of the vision and the caliber of the team inspired me. As I learned more, I knew this vision would become a reality. And to think I could use my education and professional experience to make it work; that was thrilling!

"For how I'm wired, this is the opportunity of a lifetime. There's no better feeling than knowing I'm helping people in need. This stems from the values instilled in me by my mother, Louise. And part of it is due to a life-goal adopted in early adulthood—that I would always strive to pursue peace, promote justice and respect the dignity of every human being. That goal is still my northern star and my benchmark for personal success."

Paul's concern is personal as well as humanitarian. "My sister-in-law, a niece and a nephew all wrestled with epilepsy. I've seen the life-changing difference the right medications and treatment can make. I desperately want everyone with epilepsy to have the same chance for a better future."

OWP and ROW had the usual challenges of any startups. Initial growth was slower than expected. This meant most of Paul's work was a labor of love—sweat equity in a future he was helping to create. While piloting ROW through the 501(c)(3) approval process, he also handled some regulatory issues and state approvals for OWP to sell its medications. Early on he recruited Lori Hairrell as a part-time Program Developer. She too donated a lot of time and energy to laying the groundwork for growth.

"When Paul invited me to join the ROW Foundation," Lori says with a smile, "he casually mentioned the opportunity to volunteer for an hour or so per week. I agreed, but quickly saw that with the great needs of the global epilepsy community, a few hours a week wouldn't cut it. But I was hooked. ROW's vision and mission appealed to my sense of justice."

One of Lori's main tasks has been to facilitate relationships with potential grant recipients. "We field inquiries from advocacy groups, hospitals and orphanages with epilepsy programs. With limited financial resources, we've had to be creative, but we're gaining momentum every month."

Like everyone involved with ROW, Lori has a deep desire to balance the scales when it comes to medical treatment. "To learn that millions of people around the world live with untreated epilepsy was startling," she admits. "That kind of suffering is so unnecessary. I want to connect people with epilepsy to resources that will enable them to flourish in spite of their condition."

In February 2015, ROW secured its IRS designation as a 501(c)(3) private foundation. It could now receive tax deductible contributions. Two months later, it launched an Indiegogo crowdfunding campaign to purchase EEG equipment and to prime the pump for other projects.

While ROW isn't dependent on such charitable gifts, they are always welcome. And because OWP's profits cover all general and administrative expenses, every dollar given by donors flows directly to people in need—specifically, people suffering with one of the oldest known, and most misunderstood, diseases.

The Need

*Compassion is an action word
with no boundaries.*

— Prince

For their hybrid model to work, Scott and Bruce realized there had to be a market for a product and a social need connected to that market. Epilepsy emerged as the clear choice, and a vision for improving the conditions for people with the disorder in under-resourced areas came into focus.

Epilepsy is characterized by recurrent seizures, brief episodes of involuntary shaking that involve a part of or the entire body. These seizures are a result of excessive electrical discharges in the brain. They can vary from brief lapses of atten-

tion or muscle jerks to severe and prolonged con-
vulsions.

People with epilepsy have additional physical
problems such as fractures and bruising suffered
during seizures. They have higher rates of other
disorders and psychosocial issues like anxiety and
depression. Their risk of premature death is two to
three times higher than for the general population.

Experts don't know the exact number of people living with epilepsy. It's generally accepted that
around 1 percent of the population is experiencing
epilepsy at any time. With a world population top-
ping 7.6 billion, the figure could be as high as 70
million. The World Health Organization (WHO) puts
the numbers like this:

> The estimated proportion of the general
> population with active epilepsy at a giv-
> en time is between 4 and 10 per 1000
> people. However, some studies in low-
> and middle-income countries suggest
> that the proportion is much higher, be-
> tween 7 and 14 per 1000 people. Glob-
> ally, an estimated 2.4 million people are
> diagnosed with epilepsy each year. In
> high-income countries, annual new cas-
> es are between 30 and 50 per 100,000
> people. In low- and middle-income

countries, this figure can be up to two times higher. ... Close to 80% of people with epilepsy live in low- and middle-income countries.

When it comes to the United States, a 2015 study by the Centers for Disease Control and Prevention found that about 3 million adults and 470,000 children have epilepsy. To put that number in perspective, while epilepsy has a much lower public profile than Parkinson's disease, Lou Gehrig's disease (ALS) and multiple sclerosis, it afflicts more Americans than these three disorders combined.

Epilepsy has always been surrounded by stigmas and stereotypes, with dire consequences. Women have been sterilized. People have been burned at the stake. Many were

> *... while epilepsy has a much lower public profile than Parkinson's disease, Lou Gehrig's disease (ALS) and multiple sclerosis, it afflicts more Americans than these three disorders combined.*

placed in institutions for the criminally insane. "People with epilepsy have been viewed as mentally insane, degenerate, demonic, or intellectually diminished," says Joyce Bender, founder of Bender Consulting Services and an epilepsy patient herself. "Most of this has changed, other than in third-world countries."

The social stigma surrounding epilepsy is often more devastating than the illness. It can keep people from seeking treatment so as not to be identified with the disease. Adults can be denied insurance, a driver's license, employment in certain occupations, and even barred from marriage. Children can be banned from school or from many activities. Increasing the heartbreak, epilepsy is often comorbid with psychiatric issues such as depression, anxiety, and mood disorders.

Epilepsy can be managed with anti-epileptic drugs (AEDs) to the extent that 70 percent of those who are properly treated can live fairly normal lives. But of the millions of people with epilepsy in low- and middle-income countries, only about 25 percent receive any form of treatment. In some countries, the treatment gap can be as high as 95 percent. That means in those countries only 5 of every 100 persons with epilepsy are properly diagnosed and treated.

The Need

Physicians in these countries often lack the proper equipment to detect epilepsy. And even when they can make a diagnosis, patients often don't receive proper medications because they're not available or too expensive. A WHO study on the price and affordability of AEDs in 46 countries noted that:

> Despite the availability of cost-effective antiepileptic drugs, the majority of affected individuals in resource-poor settings do not receive treatment. A recent systematic review estimated that the epilepsy "treatment gap," or the proportion of people with active epilepsy who were not receiving treatment, was >75% in low-income countries and >50% in most middle- income countries, compared to <10% in many high-income countries.

OWP's approach to the problem of epilepsy is twofold: First, it makes effective AEDs that cost patients in the United States a fraction of the equivalent patented medications. OWP released its initial drug in 2016. Roweepra® is a branded form of the generic levetiracetam, the most frequently prescribed AED in the country. Two years later, OWP put out a second drug, Subvenite®. It's a branded form of the generic lamotrigine, the second most frequently prescribed AED. Lamotrigine is also commonly prescribed for bipolar disorder. This reflects the expanded vision of OWP and ROW to improving the treatment of epilepsy and associated psychiatric disorders.

The second part of the OWP approach is helping all people get the same treatment as patients in wealthier countries. Through its unique arrangement with ROW, a significant share of company profits flow to the foundation. ROW uses the money to upgrade treatment options for epilepsy sufferers in under-resourced areas of the world—at no charge.

In ROW parlance, "under-resourced areas" refers to places that lack access to the training, diagnosis, and treatments available in developed countries. ROW avoids tags like "first world" and "third world," as these convey a sense of ranking or superiority. It prefers "developed" and "developing" as better descriptions that correlate with the availability of the latest medical treatments.

"The global inequity in care of those with epilepsy is eye-opening and gut-wrenching," ROW's founder says. "The knowledge and medicines already exist to level the field in treating this disease. We just have to summon the will and do the work to make it a reality."

The Work

Investments in the OWP/ROW social enterprise are making a demonstrable and life-changing difference in the communities they serve.

— Social Enterprise Institute, Elizabethtown College

For the first several months of ROW's existence, Paul and Lori worked on building relationships with individuals, professional groups, and associations that would help ROW better understand and carry out its mission. Internally, the emphasis was on getting key systems into place: accounting, communications, internet and social media platforms, and more. Additionally, they spent time and money creating a portfolio of written and electronic material to promote the ROW brand, explaining the new social enterprise, and educating the public about global epilepsy.

ROW's first funding project came with a $24,000 price tag. The foundation would buy electroencephalography (EEG) equipment for a pediatric hospital in Yerevan, the capital of Armenia. In April 2015, ROW launched an Indiegogo campaign to raise money for the equipment. In June it placed an order with Natus Neurology for a thirty-two-channel video EEG workstation, with computer and monitor. The equipment was delivered in July to the Arabkir Pediatric Hospital.

Dr. Biayna Sukhudyan supervised the grant. She's Chief of Neuropediatrics at the hospital and Vice President of the Armenia national chapter of the International League Against Epilepsy (ILAE). A year later, she reported the hospital had examined about 100 patients with the equipment, all of them difficult-to-treat cases. She expects to serve a similar number of patients each year going forward.

This grant is just the beginning. With the assistance of the ILAE, ROW has identified fifteen locations where EEG equipment would make a crucial difference to under-resourced populations. For the vast majority of these people, access to such equipment and to the treatment that would follow is beyond reach. ROW wants to change that.

But equipment by itself isn't enough. The second part of ROW's three-pronged approach is training physicians and healthcare workers. This might include onsite educational programs, telemedicine consultations, and workshops on EEG equipment. Where possible, a link is established with neurologists in the United States who can read the tests remotely and consult on treatment.

The third prong of the ROW strategy is donating anti-epileptic drugs (AEDs), specifically the OWP medication, Roweepra. As Paul explains, "When we enter into a partnership with healthcare providers it's a long-term commitment because epilepsy is a lifetime struggle. We don't want to start people on helpful treatment that can't be sustained. And as the need grows we'll be able to send more medication, thanks to the generosity of OWP."

Here's what this strategy looks like from the receiving end. Jolly Lux, Executive Director of Guiding Light Orphans, writes, "We appreciate ROW's commitment to bringing the best possible care to persons living with epilepsy in areas where modern diagnostic tools and treatment options just aren't available. They provided us with a grant to support our clinic operations and the purchase of needed medications. Together we're exploring ways to get newer, more effective AEDs into Uganda. The future is just a bit brighter!"

The first shipment of Roweepra went to the Arabkir United Children's Charity Foundation for the Arabkir Pediatric Hospital in Yerevan. Since then, ROW has begun supplying AEDs to hospitals and medical clinics in Bolivia, Haiti, Uganda, and Sierra Leone, as well as to several organizations in the United States. The foundation plans to provide additional grants to Tanzania, India, Rwanda, Uganda, and Kenya. It also wants to make diagnostic, research, and training grants to Ghana, India, Swaziland, and the Republic of Georgia.

ROW's projects are easy to track through the series of One-Page Updates it publishes. Here are a few excerpts that show the progress from the initial grant to the time this book went to press:

August 2016 – ROW gave a grant to Epilepsy Health Management (EHM) of Crystal Lake, Illinois, to improve the care of patients suffering with epilepsy as a result of traumatic brain injuries. EHM's telehealth platform is used for neurology appointments and to host online networking groups and education programs for patients.

September 2016 – ROW helped Dr. Peter London and his team deliver EEG equipment and training to two Kenyan hospitals. The mobile units were acquired through grants from Natus Neurology and ROW. This project served as a proof of concept for internet-based distance education and treatment.

October 2016 – The foundation sent a grant of Roweepra to Solidarity Bridge/Puente Solidaridad for use in Hospital Materno Infantil in Cochabamba, Bolivia. Solidarity Bridge trains and equips medical communities in Bolivia and Paraguay.

March 2017 – ROW began work with the Children's Hope Medical/Dental Clinic in Jacmel, Haiti. The foundation provides an ongoing supply of Roweepra for use in a region where AEDs are unavailable. With it, doctors can radically improve the lives of people living with epilepsy.

March 2017 – Dr. Peter London had a vision of taking an EEG machine into the mountains of Haiti. He came up with an ingenious design that was solar powered and portable. ROW provided Roweepra to Dr. London, as it has for his previous trips. His team visited patients in Jacmel and the mountain towns of Bossier and Cap Rouge.

September 2017 – ROW shipped a supply of Roweepra to CURE Children's Hospital in Mbale, Uganda. Subsequent shipments will follow as needed. CURE International operates ten hospitals around the world. The hospital in Uganda deals with neurological disorders, including epilepsy.

October 2017 – To address the dire need for AEDs in Puerto Rico after Hurricane Maria, ROW donated thirteen cases of Roweepra. The medication was delivered with the assistance of the Epilepsy Foundation of Greater Chicago and Dr. Rebecca Garcia Sosa of Chicago's Lurie Children's Hospital. This $35,000 worth of medication was ROW's largest grant to date.

January 2018 – ROW sent a medication grant to the Loreto Health Services Center in Makeni, Sierra Leone. The center cares for about 650 patients monthly. Services include maternal and child healthcare, immunization, and the treatment of diseases like malaria, typhoid, and epilepsy.

Spring 2018 – ROW has several projects in the pipeline to serve those in under-resourced parts of the world:

- Providing a 32-channel video EEG workstation to a neurology institute in the Republic of Georgia.
- Providing mobile EEG equipment to a pediatric hospital in India.
- Providing a training grant to launch a neurodiagnostic program at a university in Cameroon.
- Providing a training grant for healthcare workers in Nepal to aid in the diagnosis and treatment of epilepsy. This telehealth project also offers referrals for patients needing care for comorbid psychiatric conditions."

- Providing ongoing medication grants to Armenia, Bolivia, Haiti, Sierra Leone, Uganda, and the United States.

There's no question that ROW has been busy, but has it been effective? One way to measure success is by something called Social Return on Investment (SROI). SROI measures the social, environmental, and economic costs and benefits of an organization, program, or project. An SROI analysis generates a financial ratio comparing "value in" with immediate and long-term "value out." This allows investors or donors to know the economic and social benefit of their involvement.

In the spring of 2017, ROW retained the Social Enterprise Institute (SEI) at Elizabethtown College to conduct an independent SROI analysis. The analysis focused on ROW's Kenya Mobile EEG Project. It considered the SROI for ROW's contribution to the project, as well as the SROI for the larger enterprise of OWP and ROW together. Two ratios were generated:

1. A ratio of $4.95 return to $1.00 investment, representing the SROI for the social enterprise entity of OWP and ROW together.
2. A ratio of $57.54 return to $1.00 investment, representing the SROI for ROW's donor dollars paid into the project.

(Although the analysis considered a one-year period, the project is expected to yield long-term benefits well into the future.)

One aspect of ROW's Standard Operating Procedure is apparent from its short history: ROW believes in the power of teamwork.

The Partners

There are many quality organizations assisting people with epilepsy. What distinguishes ROW from the others is two-fold. First, most other organizations are heavily dependent on grants and donations. The OWP/ROW structure frees the foundation from the time-and-cost-intensive effort to find, win over, and retain donors. Instead, it is funded by the profitability of OWP.

Second, ROW is a funding foundation, not an operating foundation. It fulfills its mission by supporting well-established organizations with proven programs. ROW isn't interested in re-inventing the wheel; it exists to grease the ones that are effectively rolling so as to cover more territory.

ROW has established partnerships with key international organizations, including:

> *ROW isn't interested in reinventing the wheel; it exists to grease the ones that are effectively rolling so as to cover more territory.*

- » The World Health Organization (WHO)
- » International League Against Epilepsy (ILAE)
- » The International Bureau for Epilepsy (IBE)
- » World Federation for Mental Health (WFMH)
- » World Psychiatric Association (WPA)
- » Epilepsy Foundation of America (EFA) and its state and regional chapters and affiliates

Working smarter often means partnering with others by pooling resources and expertise to reach common goals. In a conversation with the president of the ILAE, Paul mentioned ROW's intent to do a study on the diagnostic equipment and AEDs available around the world to determine the areas of greatest need.

"He told me the ILAE, WHO and the International Bureau for Epilepsy were jointly working on just such a report," Paul recounts. "It didn't make sense to do our research when these larger organizations had already undertaken this strategic project. Instead we made a financial gift to their study, which will help us prioritize our projects in the coming years."

Many medical professionals in remote and impoverished settings are thrilled about what ROW adds to the healthcare equation. "We've been in dialogue with ROW and we're excited about a partnership that will enhance basic neurological services through our hospitals in rural North India," says Sunil Gokavi, MD, President of Emmanuel Hospital Association (India). "ROW's focus on sustainable, humanitarian service fits well with our efforts to diagnose and treat epilepsy. We will obtain the services of a neurologist at one of our locations by the middle of 2018, so an EEG machine becomes more relevant for us!"

Around the world and at home, ROW is cultivating relationships with leading epileptologists (specialists in treating epilepsy), neurologists, and psychiatrists—the latter because epilepsy is often combined with various psychiatric disorders. Several leading experts serve on the board of directors or advisory board:

▶ Marvin A. Rossi, MD, PhD, Associate Professor and Co-Director of the Multimodality Neuroimaging and Neuroengineering Laboratory at the Rush Epilepsy Center at Rush University Medical Center in Chicago.

....

▶ Patricia A. Gibson, M.S., Associate Professor in the Department of Neurology at Wake Forest University School of Medicine. She also serves as Director of the Epilepsy Information Service and as Executive Director of the Epilepsy Foundation of North Carolina.

....

▶ Aashit Shah, MD, Professor of Neurology at Wayne State University School of Medicine and Director of its Comprehensive Epilepsy Program. He is also Chief of Neurology at Harper University Hospital.

....

▶ Samuel O. Okpaku, MD, PhD, Founder of the Center for Health, Culture and Society in Nashville. He was Clinical Professor of Psychiatry at Vanderbilt University Medical

School and Chairman of the Department of Psychiatry, Meharry Medical School, in Nashville.

....

▶ Emilio Perucca, MD, PhD, Past-President of the ILAE. He is Professor of Pharmacology at University of Pavia Medical School and Director of the Clinical Trial Centre at the C. Mondino National Neurological Institute in Pavia, Italy.

....

▶ Kurt Florian, JD, was a partner at prestigious law firms in Chicago. His childhood experiences with seizures, as well his daughter's epilepsy, led him to serve on the board of the Epilepsy Foundation of Greater Chicago for more than twenty years.

Other experts are catching the OWP/ROW vision and bringing their skills and resources to the movement. One example is Keith Morgan, founder of Neurotech EEG Specialists. "I met Scott and Paul, and through them I got connected to a neurologist planning trips to Kenya and Haiti. I've been able to do detailed training sessions via web conferences with the techs he trained in Kenya. Teleconferencing is great, but I believe training is best done in person. That's why Neurotech has designated money, equipment and staff to follow our EEG machines into the field."

ROW isn't interested in credit or control in these relationships. It doesn't have to impress donors or elbow out other organizations for a share of the philanthropic pie. It has no problem playing a supporting role because it doesn't have competitors, only comrades in a common cause: to provide "the highest attainable standard of health" to everyone struggling with epilepsy and associated psychiatric disorders.

The "WHY"

WHY is the thing that inspires us
and inspires those around us.

— Simon Sinek

"Any person or organization can explain what they do," writes Simon Sinek in his book Start With Why. "Some can explain how they are different or better; but very few can clearly articulate why. WHY is not about money or profit—those are results. WHY is the thing that inspires us and inspires those around us."

ROW's "why" is very clear. It is laser-focused on improving conditions related to epilepsy and associated psychiatric disorders in under-resourced regions. It provides funding for projects that fulfill its mission in cooperation with other epilepsy-related entities. "We measure our success by the amount of funding we're able to generate," Paul explains. "And by how many lives we help change for the better. Not only will we know when we hit the bull's-eye, but others will know it as well. Our detailed financials are available to the public. That's how it should be."

The ROW Foundation seeks to define itself by intentional action, measurable accomplishment and organizational transparency. It faces two main challenges on the road ahead: how to coordinate the healthcare professionals in the United States who want to help; and how to address the requests for assistance.

"There's far more to do than we presently have resources for," Paul explains. "That will change as OWP becomes more profitable and ROW receives more revenue from the company. I believe our model will allow us to become the world's largest funder of projects serving people with epilepsy. But presently we're counting each dollar and applying it as strategically as we possibly can."

And as for the man behind the vision, Scott reflects, "I'm not certain why I began asking questions about the social injustice behind the 'ROW' designation. Perhaps it was my age, the time in my career, or the fact that my wife and I were entering the empty nest phase. Whatever the reasons, I felt like I had to do something.

This undertaking is in uncharted territory. Those of us who have started it have a lot of our own time and money on the line. This is the riskiest, and the most exciting, thing I've ever done. It makes me want to get up every morning. And every night when I go to bed I think about the ongoing impact and lasting legacy this new social enterprise can have."

The ultimate goal of the ROW Foundation is to improve the lives

This undertaking is in uncharted territory. Those of us who have started it have a lot of our own time and money on the line. This is the riskiest, and the most exciting, thing I've ever done.

of millions of people with epilepsy who are sitting on the sidelines of life hoping to get into the game. New diagnostic equipment and treatment methods don't have to be invented to reach those living beyond the horizon of modern medicine. What's been missing is a means of distribution that's self-supporting and scalable.

Not anymore.

The OWP/ROW hybrid represents a paradigm shift in healthcare for billions of under-served people in ROW countries and millions more in the United States, where prescription costs are often astronomical. Their model proves there's more than enough margin in pharmaceuticals to provide a healthy profit and help those in need. What they're doing for epilepsy patients can be done for people dealing with cancer, heart disease, diabetes, and a myriad of other disorders.

The World Health Organization's Constitution sees "the highest attainable standard of health as a fundamental right of every human being." Anything less is inhuman, as Martin Luther King Jr. said: "Of all the forms of inequality, injustice in healthcare is the most shocking and inhuman."

ROW believes this injustice can be remedied. "One World, One Standard" is possible if enough good people decide to make it so.

Act as if what you do makes a difference. It does.

— William James

Compassionate Care
Worldwide

OWP
Pharmaceuticals

ROW
Foundation

For more information:
www.rowpharma.org
www.facebook.com/rowglobal
www.owppharma.com

Meet the Author

Mike Hamel

I've been a storyteller all my life and a full-time writer since 1996. Along the way I've published more than twenty books, including a trilogy on entrepreneurs and executives. I've edited other business books such as *Serving Two Masters* by C. William Pollard, former CEO of ServiceMaster. For younger readers I've written the Matterhorn the Brave series and the TLC series. You can find all my titles on my Amazon Author Page: www.amazon.com/-/e/B001JSB7FE.